Natural objects and scents always bring a touch of the outdoors into our homes.
Add naturals to your candles... a sense of harmony with all creation is instantly yours.

Easy Projects ▶

Nature's Way... Add Natural Elements

1. Pick dried naturals and decide on placement. Place in container with the wick.

2. Pour gel. Some naturals will bubble a lot. Skim the bubbles off the top with a spoon.

Butterflies - Position Red and Yellow feather butterflies. Place small amount of cool Yellow gel in one corner to form a hazy color as hot gel melts it. Add the gel slowly.

Oranges & Spice - Add dried oranges, cinnamon sticks and cloves to Clear gel. The color comes from spices.

Dried Flowers - Dry daisies or mums. Add Pale Pink gel.

Cinnamon Sticks - Line sides of straight-sided holder with cinnamon sticks. Pour 1" of gel and make sure sticks stand. Allow to cool. Pour additional Clear gel to top.

Maple Leaf - Use pressed dried leaf, dried Red berries and acorns. Place berries and acorns in bottom and pour Clear gel. Make sure elements do not float. Place leaf against side of glass away from the flame. Gradate pale Blue while filling candle.

Cardinals - Pour Pale Green about ¼" up. Place small stick and one bird in place. When cool, fill pot and add other bird. You may have to keep them from floating.

more on... Candle Making Basics

Submerging Objects - Submerge innumerable objects in the gel wax. Objects must be resistant to burning and melting. Add things such as marbles, buttons, toys and jewels. Silk leaves may be used but must be kept away from the flame. Do not use highly flammable items. Some objects will float, so add the items as the gel cools and thickens. Continually keep pushing items down with craft sticks and knife blades or they may float to the top. Be aware some items will bubble and fall apart, so you may want to do some tests before using them. This is fun and creative for kids!

Heating Wax - Paraffin should be heated to 130° to 140°F. The gel wax melting point is between 160° and 170°F. Always use a double boiler for paraffin wax. If you do not have a double boiler, use a smaller pan submerged in water contained in a larger pan. Heat the gel wax directly on the burner set at medium to low heat. Tear the gel into small pieces to help control the amount of bubbles.

Precautions - Always use the utmost care when melting wax. It is highly flammable. Work in a properly ventilated area. Never leave melting wax unattended. It is handy to keep an open box of baking soda nearby while heating wax. Never try to use water on a wax fire. Smother the fire with baking soda and a pan lid. Paraffin will ignite at about 400°F. It is a good idea to never let wax heat over 200F.

Clean Up - Use dish soap and hot water to clean gel from utensils, counter tops and tools. Paraffin cleans by running under hot water then soapy water. Scrape off hardened wax on counter tops and wash with soapy water. Turpentine can be used to dissolve small amounts of wax on counter tops.

Down by the Sea

What can be more enjoyable than a day at the seashore? Bring back the joy all year long with candles filled with memories from the beach.

Starfish - Add 1" of sea glass on bottom. Pour Pale Blue gel and add starfish next to side.

Fish & Sand Layers - Tilt jar and add colored sand. Change direction of tilt for each color of sand. Be careful not to disturb existing sand. End with Black across top. Bury wick in sand by punching down with a knife point to bottom. Place shells. Pour Clear melted gel to cover shells being careful to not disturb sand. Allow to set until cool. Shells may float, so keep in place with a knife tip. Add gel almost to top. When starting to thicken, add plastic fish. Press fish in position next to glass to help keep in place. Fish will try to float. When completely cool, add a layer of Blue paraffin.

Shells & Star - Fill tall glass jar half full with small shells. Pour Clear gel to cover shells. Add more Clear gel with a little Blue to top. Position the starfish in place using a knife tip.

Conch Shell - Decide how shell will sit before starting. Place wick and pour very Light Blue gel. This would make a pretty addition to a pool party.

Fishing in a Bowl - Pour in sand. Add shells. Position a silk plant away from wick. Bowl will have to be large or eliminate plant. Hang hook and tape line to jar lip. Pour Clear gel in slowly. Make sure plant remains in place using knife. As thickening begins, add plastic fish next to glass side. It may float and expand, so keep punching with a knife.

Dollar in Sand - Pour sand in bottom to a third full. Place sea glass and shells. Pour Pale Blue gel for another third. Allow to thicken, add sand dollar. Partially thicken. Pour rest of the gel to top.

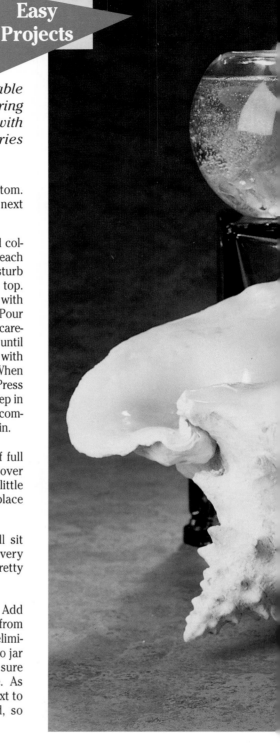

Down by the Sea Instructions

Submerging Objects Tip

• Continually keep pushing items down with craft sticks and knife blades or they may float to the top.

1. Place wick in container.

2. Arrange shells as desired.

3. Pour wax over shells. Make sure shells do not float. Fill container to top.

Bottoms Up... Faux Drink Candles

Easy Projects

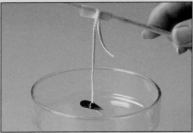

Basic Candle Instructions

Prepare container. Choose a glass or acrylic container. Fill with water and pour into measuring cup to determine amount of gel needed. As you become proficient at using the gel, you can just melt and pour.

Prepare wick. Measure and cut wick about 3" longer than glass is tall. Thread wick through metal wick clip base and crimp with pliers. Place metal base down into candle container hanging other end of the wick out of container. You can substitute a small washer for the metal base. You will need a craft stick or pencil handy to center wick after pouring melted gel. Always put wick in first before wax.

Prepare gel wax. Crumble gel and add to level of water in measuring cup. Add more if necessary while heating.

Heat Gel. Clip candy thermometer in pan and add wax. Heat on a medium low burner until all wax is melted. *Do not* leave unattended. *Do not* place in microwave.

Dye. Add dye color of choice while wax is melting. Shave off small amounts. You need very little. It is easy to get wax too dark and lose the transparent quality. You can also use pre-colored gel pieces as part of the coloring process.

Add scent just before pouring.

Pour melted gel wax. Hold back bubbles with a knife or spoon if you do not want them in candle. For some containers, it is best to allow the gel to cool a little before pouring.

Center wick and place craft stick across top of glass to keep it in position.

Champagne - Yellow + pinch of Brown dye. Place Clear chunks in bottom of glass. Pour melted gel.

Cappuccino - Place coffee beans in bottom third of mug. Pour Brown gel, cool. Whip wax for whipping cream (See page 8 for whipping instructions.) and dab on top.

Wine - Use a wine glass and Red + Purple dye.

Ice - Crumble gel and place in a glass with wick.

Ice Tea - Pour Clear then Pale Reddish Brown. Insert dried orange slice.

Hot Tea - Reddish Brown. Insert Cinnamon stick when gel begins to thicken.

Margarita - Pour Pale Green gel then Clear and Pale Yellow. Spread whipped paraffin wax on edge of glass for salt.

Ice Cube & Gelatin Instructions

1. Spray some cooking spray into the mold and wipe out any excess.

Create outstanding works of candle art using clear gel. Clear wax broadens the scope of what you can do with this art form. These candles will last longer than paraffin candles and add hours of pleasing aroma and glowing enjoyment to your home.

Helpful Tips

● Crumbling gel wax helps to control bubbles and aids in consistent heating.

● Placing wax ice cubes in the freezer for 15 minutes will prevent melting as you pour hot gel over them.

● Remember that gel is hotter temperature than paraffin wax, so allow it to cool some before pouring on paraffin.

Melt gel. Add 3 tablespoons of stearic acid or White colorant to turn opaque White.

3. Pour the melted gel into the pan, harden and cut 1" cubes.

5. Place frozen gel cubes in glass along with wick.

6. Melt and pour the gel around the cubes. Allow the hot gel to cool some before pouring.

Whipped Wax Instructions

This method is used for whipping cream, ice cream and icing. Whipped wa... is made from paraffin only. Gel will not work for whipping.
Note - ¹/₂ cup of wax makes one dip of ice cream.

1. Heat paraffin in a double boiler. Add color and scent.

2. Pour hot wax into a deep bowl. Whip vigorously using a whisk or electric mixer to form fluffy froth. Whip until almost cool and to consistency of whipping cream. Whip longest for ice cream. If wax becomes too hard to work, reheat and repeat process.

3. Working quickly, spray an ice crea... scoop with cooking spray and scoop w... for ice cream dips. Use a spoon to a... whipped toppings.

Easy Projects

Safety Precaution

Always use the utmost care when melting wax. It is highly flammable. Work in a properly ventilated area. Never leave melt-ing wax unattended. It is handy to keep an open box of baking soda while heating wax. Never try to use water on a wax fire. Smother the fire with baking soda and a pan lid. Paraffin will ignite at about 400°F. It is recommended to never let wax heat over 200F.

Too Good to Eat... Dessert Candles for Every Occasion

Easy Projects

Brownie Delight - Pour Brown gel in a greased pan ¾" deep. When cool, cut into 3" square and place on a saucer for brownie. Whip paraffin wax for ice cream. Allow to cool to room temperature. Place in freezer for 15 minutes before adding Pink gel. Melt, allow to cool and drizzle Pink on ice cream. Top with a cherry. Find a small half circle to mold cherry.

Red Jello - Pour Red gel into a greased small metal container 1" deep. Allow to cool, remove and cut into cubes. Place jello blocks in small bowl and pour clear gel around cubes.

Cup Cakes - Place foiled cupcake paper in a supporting holder and have ready. Pour melted Pink in one and Brown for chocolate in other paper, filling to the top. Allow to cool. Mound whipped paraffin in matching color on top of cupcakes to add height. Add a little more gel on top for icing, but allow gel to cool before adding to the cake or cake may melt.

Ice Cream Dream - Whip Brown paraffin adding a hint of Red and Pink. Follow the instructions for Brownie and drizzle the Brown gel for chocolate syrup.

Parfait - Crumble Red gel in the bottom of a parfait glass and add wick. Have next layer of Red jello ready. Whip wax. Add layer of whipped cream then Jello and top with whipped cream. Work fast. Pull wick taut.

Yellow Jello - Pour Pale Yellow in a small glass bowl. Do not get color too dark or gel will not be transparent.

Gel Candles Color Guide

Red + Yellow = Orange
Blue + Yellow = Green
Red + Blue = Purple
Green + Yellow = Lime Green
Green + Yellow + pinch of Brown = Olive Green
3 parts Brown + 1 part Red = Reddish Brown
2 parts Yellow + 1 part Green = Yellow Green
5 parts Yellow +1 part Reddish Brown = Amber

Rich, jeweled colors give these warm glowing candles a look all their own.

Stained Glass Candle Instructions

Advanced Projects

1. Spray oil on a non-stick cookie sheet. Melt gel and add color. Dark colors work best. Pour 1/16" to 1/8" layer on cookie sheet.

2. When cool, pull up and store on wax paper. Repeat for every color used. Make a clear gel sheet.

3. Cut Clear gel sheet to inside dimensions of one wall of container. To control drag, oil knife blade. Create design on Clear sheet. When colored gel sheets are cool, place pattern under gel and cut out with a straight knife. Place pieces on top of Clear sheet of gel using pattern as a guide. Press out air bubbles between layers of gel.

4. Using a knife, slide designed piece into container with Clear sheet next to container wall. Press out the air bubbles. Repeat on remaining sides. Place a wick in the container. Heat paraffin in a double boiler. Add scent but no color. Pour slowly trying not to pour on gel. Fill container. After cooling, add additional paraffin.

Safety Precaution

Always use the utmost care when melting wax. It is highly flammable. Work in a properly ventilated area. Never leave melting wax unattended. It is handy to keep an open box of baking soda while heating wax. Never try to use water on a wax fire. Smother the fire with baking soda and a pan lid. Paraffin will ignite at about 400°F. It is recommended to never let wax heat over 200F.

Cut Out Shapes... Stained Glass Effects

Red Flower - Cut Red flower, Green leaves and Amber shapes. Make paraffin Light Yellow.

Butterflies - Cut Pink butterfly, Blue wavy shape, Green grass, Yellow and Blue stripes and Pink and Green circles. Cut circles using a scent bottle lid.

Tulips - Cut Red tulip, Green leaves, Pale Amber background, Dark Green stripe and Green and Yellow grass blades. Repeat flower and grass on additional sides.

Christmas Tree - Cut Green Christmas tree and circles with a scent bottle lid. Add colored gel to spots. Cut Gold snowflake. Add sequin on top. Cut Blue packages with 2 Green circles for bows and Red package with 2 triangles for bow.

Fun Fruit - Cut Purple grapes using a scent bottle lid as a cookie cutter, Green leaves, Yellow with a bit of Amber pear, odd Red, Green and Yellow shapes. Repeat design on 4 sides or use irregular shapes in same color scheme.

Stained Glass Chips - Place colored gel chunks on a cookie sheet. Pour hot gel on chips to meld them. Place cooled sheet around jar edge. Press out air bubbles. Fill with paraffin.

Funky Cube - Make Light Red, Brown, Red, Pale Lime Green and Yellow sheets. Cut small various size rectangles for each row.

*Stained Glass Candle Patterns
Continued on page 12*

How to Layer Colors

There are 2 methods used to layer, one produces distinct stripes of colors while the other creates a smooth gradation of color. These methods can be used for both paraffin and gel wax. There is less distinction of layers using gel. Keep in mind that the colors will visually blend because of the transparent nature of the gel. Do not put contrasting colors together or you will get muddy colors. If you pour a second color of gel on a first layer that has not cooled, the 2 layers will mix to form a new wax color.

Layers of Color

1. Prepare container and decide colors to layer. Melt gel, add color and scent. Pour hot gel into container. Allow to cool and harden.

2. Pour in second layer, cool and harden.

3. Repeat for as many layers as desired.

4. Tilt container for different layering shapes.

Smooth Gradated Colors

1. Prepare container, add wick.
2. Heat wax for darkest color using double amount so Clear wax may be added later to lighten color. Add dye.
3. Pour darkest layer first and allow to harden. For good gradation, do not fill more than a fourth full.
4. Add an additional amount of Clear wax to the wax remaining from step 2 to lighten the color. Melt and add to the first layer.
5. Repeat step 4 as many times as necessary ending with Clear. You do not have to wait till gel is completely cooled, just thickened. Repeat gradation to dark again by reversing process from Clear to dark.

Beautiful Layered Luminaries

Colors changing from dark to light… these elegant candles add a rainbow touch to any room. Make some in different colors then group them together for a brilliantly glowing arrangement.

Tall Red - Pour Wine + Red for ¾", let harden. Follow Gradation Instructions. Add a little Yellow to Red at the top.

Snow Flakes - 5 Blue sequin snowflakes. Pour dark Blue for 1". Layer and suspend snowflakes. It helps to press snowflakes against glass to hold in position. Top off last ½" with Blue.

Pink Flower Pot - Pour Wine Red. If dye is unavailable, mix 3 parts Red to 1 part Blue. Pour bottom half and top with Clear. Cool Wine Red to prevent color mixture.

Diagonally Layered - Tilt jar and pour Wine Red. Allow to set and pour Olive Green. Allow to harden. Place jar flat on bottom and add Yellow, allow to harden. Add Wine Red to top.

Vertical Stripe Cube - Pour ¾" of Green in a small pan, allow to harden. Remove and cut 2 pieces to fill one third of candleholder leaving ½" at top. Place and press Green pieces on either side and leave center open. Melt and pour cooled Yellow in center. Allow to cool and harden. Top with Wine Red.

Fluted Blue - Layer Blue, cool a bit but not totally and add partially cooled Yellow. The Blue and Yellow combine to make Green. Layer Pale Blue on top. Pour hot gel on partially cooled gel to mix colors a bit. Experiment with amount of heat to melting ratio.

Stained Glass Candle Patterns Continued From page 11

Painted Candle Holders

MATERIALS: Small soft paintbrush • Pebe[...] Glass Paint (Citrine, Pepper Red, Lazuli, Ear[...] Brown, Amaranthine Purple, Peridot, Blac[...] Olivine Green, Orange, White)

1. Pick out container. Use a smooth surface glass. Position and tape the pattern to the inside of the glass.

2. Paint design. A dabbing motion works better than strokes. For corrections, wait till tacky and scrape off with fingernail. Paint smears if corrections are made while wet. Bake the paint following the manufacturer's instructions.

3. Pour the candle using a very pale g[...] wax color.

Painting on glass candleholders is fun! Get everyone in the family involved. The kids will especially enjoy these quick and simple paint projects. If you make a mistake just scrape it off. What could be easier?

Smiley - Paint face Black. Fill with Yellow gel.

Bees - Amaranthine and Citrine. Using script liner brush, dab paint on. Allow Amaranthine to dry before adding Citrine. Pour Clear gel with a ¼" square of solid Blue gel placed at bottom back. The Blue piece will melt and may be swirled.

Ladybug & Butterfly - Paint ladybug Pepper Red, allow to dry, paint Black. Paint butterfly Lazuli, outline with Amaranthine. Paint zigzag line Citrine. Fill with Clear gel.

Flower Pot - Paint wide Olivine Green line and thin Amaranthine line for plaid. Paint flowers Citrine and Amaranthine. Fill with Clear gel.

Pumpkin Head - Paint face Black with White teeth. Fill with Orange gel.

Dragonflies - Paint bodies, wings Lazuli. Paint grass Peridot and dab flowers Pepper Red. Fill with Clear gel.

Violets - Paint flowers Amaranthine with Citrine centers. Leaves and stems Olivine Green. Fill with Pink gel.

Snowman - Paint eyes Black and nose Orange. Crumble gel into the holder to three-quarters full, pour in hot gel.

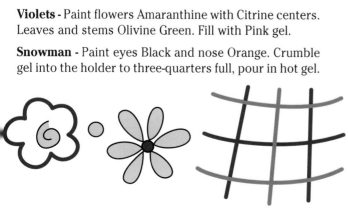

Gel in Terra Cotta Patio Pots

1. Spray the mold with cooking oil spray.

2. Pour the colored paraffin in the mold, let it harden and pop out of mold.

3. Paint with acrylic paint.

4. Place the wicks in the terra cotta saucer, add gel, cool and place the turtles.

Ladybug Social - Make 6 ladybugs using plastic Easter egg for mold. Pour melted Yellow gel in a 5½" terra cotta saucer. Cool and place ladybugs on top.

Turtle Tunes - Make 3 Lime Green turtles using Life of the Party mold. Paint eyes with acrylic paint. Pour melted Green gel in a 6" terra cotta saucer. Place turtles after gel sets.

Frog Friends - Make 3 Green frogs using Life of the Party mold. Paint eyes and mouth with acrylic paint. Pour melted Blue gel in a 4" terra cotta saucer. Place the frogs just before the gel sets firm.

Butterfly Pot - Pour melted Green gel in a 3½" terra cotta pot. Place the doubled butterfly wire in the pot as the gel thickens.

Wiry Pot - Pour melted Pink gel in a 3" terra cotta pot. Place Gold and Red spiraled wires in the pot as the gel thickens.

Flower in a Pot - Pour melted Pink gel in a 2" terra cotta pot. Place the wire in the pot as the gel thickens. Keep the flower away from flame.

Make a collection of nature friendly candles for your next patio party. From frogs to ladybugs and flowers to butterflies, every creation will be the talk of your party.

Suspend fun objects in your candles for a whimsical look.